Manners During the Civil War:

American Etiquette, or the Customs

Adopted by Polite Society throughout the

United States

Edited and with notes by

Michelle L. Hamilton

THE SALUTATION.

MLH Publications
12771 Camellia Drive
Ruther Glen VA 22546

American Etiquette, or the Customs Adopted by Polite Society Throughout the United States first published in the United States by John Murphy and Company 1850. This edition with an introduction by Michelle L. Hamilton published in MLH Publications 2017.

Library of Congress Cataloging–in-Publication Data

Hamilton, Michelle L.
"Manners During the Civil War; American Etiquette, or The Customs Adopted by Polite Society Throughout the United States.
(2017)

ISBN: 978-0-9995688-0-4

Illustration
Title Page—"The Salutation" from Thomas Hillgrove, *Hillgrove's Ball Room Guide and Practical Dancer*, Dick & Fitzgerald, New York, 1863, pg. 57.

Editor's Introduction

In the 16th-century, scholar William Horman wrote that "manners maketh man." Nearly four hundred years later, manners and etiquette were still viewed as essential. Before the American Revolution, an individual's social and economic standing was dependent upon the class into which he or she had been born into. A common laborer would never be able to rise economically from the working class to become a member of the gentry. Manners were indicators of the class a person was born into. In the American colonies the manners of the gentry were closely modeled after the manners found in aristocratic England. These manners separated the gentry from the coarser manners of the lower classes. Following the American Revolution, the aristocratic manners of the American gentry were quickly abandoned for the republican manners befitting a democratic society.

With the growth of industry and the settlement of the West in the United States the middle class grew. For the first time in American history, an individual could rise above the economic class into which he or she had been born into. This growth presented a quandary for the growing middle class, how to behave in this new society? Out of this need for etiquette, guide writers produced scores of manuals to help ease the transition into the middle class. Most of these etiquette manuals were copied from similar volumes published in England. Naturally, these etiquette manuals reflected European manners and ideology. In response to these volumes an anonymous author wrote *American Etiquette, or the Customs Adopted by Polite Society throughout the United States* in 1850. The book was published by the Baltimore, Maryland publisher John Murphy & Co. For whatever reason, the author chose to remain anonymous, but was clearly a member of the upper class. Throughout the pages of *American Etiquette* the author showed a familiarity with the manners and modes of society in both the North and the South which would have only been possible through extensive travel.

Written in a clear and concise manner, *American Etiquette* stands out as an excellent example of 19th-century etiquette guides. As an historian, I was thrilled to discovery this book and felt that it would be of interest to others as a time capsule of American manners during the Civil War era. On the following pages I have faithfully reproduced *American Etiquette* including the spelling and grammar which reflect the original printed in 1850.

Contents

Introduction

GOOD breeding is every where the same, and the essential requisites that go to form the true lady and gentleman of the most polished court in Europe, are no less necessary in the more simple, yet not less refined society of America.

These requisites do not reside in the chance acquisition of wealth, or the ability to make a grand display of wealth, and give large entertainments, but in those accomplishments which place their possessors at ease among those with whom they may chance to be thrown, and render courteous and agreeable companions to all who come in contact with them. Nothing has a more direct tendency to produce this result, in a naturally well disposed mind, than an exact acquaintance with the rules of good society, which are both simple and practical. It has been the purpose of the writer, in the annexed pages, to give these in the most concise and explicit manner, so as to furnish a clear guide for those who are not accustomed to its usage, as well as to those who are.

Customs Of
Polite Society In The United States.

Acquaintanceship

THERE are three modes of forming acquaintances: —
1st, by letter of introduction; 2d, by a personal introduction;
and 3d, by dispensing with these forms and meeting upon
common ground.

Letters of Introduction. — There is perhaps no
civilized country on the globe, where letters of introduction
meet with a more cold and uncertain return than in the
United States, and so doubtful is their reception that many
gentlemen decline to present them altogether.

A letter of introduction implies an acquaintance with
the person introduced on the part of the introducer, and a
belief of his fitness to be introduced into the society of the
friend to whom he introduces him, and asks this much for
him. But the bearer of the letter may find the position of the
person to whom he brings it such as not to make this

acquaintance desirable, or the individual to whom the letter is brought may have sufficient reason for wishing to dispense with this form.

Each of these ends may be accomplished, and all the parties rid of a very unpleasant dilemma, without violating any principle of etiquette, by the observance of a few simple rules, which generally obtain among well bred persons.

A letter of introduction should be unsealed, or if sealed, it should be done by the person it introduces.

It is a frequent custom to present letters of introduction in person. This method is, for many reasons, a highly objectionable one. During the perusal of the letter, a pause of great awkwardness to both parties necessarily occurs. The reader endeavors to find out the person who presents it, whilst the bearer appears to be waiting to receive such passing civilities as he sees fit to bestow, which, from the circumstances of the case, are necessarily of the coldest and most formal kind.

This may be avoided by sending the letter, with a card and address, by a messenger, to the person to whom it is directed. If he does not visit you in a very short time, you may rest assured that he would have paid little attention to you if you had presented it, and you may congratulate yourself at having escaped an unpleasant dilemma.

The receiver of a letter of introduction is bound to visit the person who bears it at once, as he offers an indignity both to the writer and bearer by allowing it to pass unnoticed. If his time is occupied, he may send his card.

The bearer of the letter may return this visit in person or by card, as he is inclined, the following day.

Thus much is due to civility; but as yet no real steps have been made towards a friendly acquaintance. It now remains for the individual to whom the letter was addressed to determine whether he wishes to cultivate the acquaintance thus offered to him. If not, he is at liberty to allow the matter to drop here. If, on the contrary, he is disposed to continue the acquaintance, he may either renew his visit or invite him to dinner, or to an evening party, or simply to his house, or show his good wishes in such manner as is most compatible with his circumstances and the supposed wishes of his new friend. This second overture is an avowed declaration of his part of a desire to continue the acquaintance.

It is now placed at the option of the person introduced to determine whether *he* wishes to continue the acquaintance. If *not*, he fails to return the second visit made to him, or declines the dinner or other civility offered. If he is desirous of continuing the acquaintance, he returns the visit or accepts the civility, and thus expresses *his* desire to become friends. Etiquette makes this first visit one of mere formality, the second one of real friendship.

Business letters, on the contrary should be presented in person. The business is sufficient apology.

One cannot be too cautious in giving a letter of introduction. He should not only be well known to the person to whom it is addressed, but should likewise take very good care that the individual introduced is a fit person to be received into the society of his friend.

More circumspection should be used in giving a gentleman a letter to a lady, than on ordinary occasions.

If a lady receives a letter introducing another lady, she should call upon her immediately, but if the letter introduces a gentleman, she may address him a note inviting him to call upon her at a specified time.

Personal Introductions — Many persons are in the habit of introducing their acquaintances to each other on all occasions, while others never introduce them.

Whatever may be the usage of other countries, the custom prevails in this of introducing those persons to each other whom the introducer is well assured will be mutually pleased with the acquaintance.

Individuals may be so circumstanced as to be placed in a very unpleasant situation unless made acquainted; or their habits, modes of thought, and position in society may be so obviously similar, as to place the propriety of the introduction beyond a question. In cases of this character an introduction is no more than a mere act of politeness, which it would be rude to overlook.

Great circumspection is necessary in introductions, in order to avoid unpleasant results. A bare casual meeting furnishes no reason for an introduction. If the wishes of the parties are not previously ascertained, (which is always best,) the individual introducing should consider well the propriety of the introduction, and having once settled this point in his own mind, it becomes his duty to introduce his friends to each other.

Always introduce the gentleman to the lady, and not the lady to the gentleman, and a person of less distinction to one of a higher position.

In introducing one individual to another, the person who does it, should be careful to mention the name of each party distinctly, with a word or two of explanation if they are entirely unknown to each other, as Mr. B. allow me to make you acquainted with Mr. R.

Mr. B. is an extensive commission merchant of Boston, Mr. R. a lawyer of some eminence. This at once supplies the parties with a knowledge of the position and modes of thought of each other.

If the name is not distinctly understood, it should be asked immediately, as, "I beg pardon, did you say Mr. B?"

As an acquaintance, when once formed, cannot be slighted except formed, cannot be slighted except for sufficient cause, without a gross departure from true politeness, it is very important to be careful in making one.

Acquaintance is a much more important consideration with ladies than gentlemen, and for this reason they are, or should be, more careful in making it.

As a general rule it is better for a lady to decline all introductions about which there is the slightest possibility of doubt, as she cannot so easily shake off an improper acquaintance, without some publicity.

Should she feel disposed to do so, it is better to decline seeing him or her, as politely as possible, so as to avoid the charge of rudeness, but even this must be encountered rather than keep up an acquaintance which might affect her injuriously.

No one is authorized to present a gentleman to a lady without first obtaining her consent, or knowing positively that it will be agreeable to her. A departure from this rule would be considered a breach of good manners, at which she would have cause to be offended.

It is not proper to take an acquaintance to the house of a friend without having first ascertained that it will be entirely agreeable. Care should be taken to explain *exactly* who the person to be introduced is, and your relations with him. There is no more effectual mode of alienating the friendship a family may entertain for an intimate acquaintance, than by his presuming upon this acquaintance, to introduce his friends into their house, without previous authority.

It is frequently said, that an acquaintance worth having is worth seeking for; and this, as a general rule, is true. But innumerable instances occur where apparently casual introductions lead to much more open and unreserved friendship, than where the knowledge exists that one or the other party took much trouble in procuring it. This, of course, implies a previous knowledge of each other.

It sometimes becomes necessary to perform the unpleasant duty, of ridding oneself of a disagreeable or improper acquaintance, and in no situation is true politeness more necessary than in this. The object is not to produce an open rupture, but simply to inform the proscribed person of a desire for a discontinuance of the acquaintance, which can usually be accomplished by an adherence, more rigid than ordinary, to the strict observances of ceremony. If he is too dull to observe this, more decided measures are warrantable, but in all cases it must be kept in view, that true good breeding is to be sustained, and no mode adopted which will detract from the character of the perfect gentleman.

A person whose acquaintance it becomes necessary to discontinue is not worthy of a quarrel, but a slight offered to a personal friend, demands an apology or reparation. The true gentleman always takes great pleasure in adopting the first method.

Unceremonious Introductions — There is no impropriety in dispensing with a formal introduction, if a person is found ready to meet another under circumstances which places the propriety of the acquaintance beyond a question, but one cannot be too careful in forming acquaintances among strangers, especially in places of public resort.

Affability is a distinctive characteristic of politeness, and frequently leads to a very unrestrained conversation among strangers when thrown together, but this cannot be considered as an approach to acquaintanceship, and should be forgotten, with the moment it served to enliven, except a mutual desire is expressed to continue the acquaintance.

Visits of Ceremony

On the arrival of a family in town, it is usual for them to announce the fact to their friends by sending their cards. This custom has many advantages. A family may be desirous of not immediately receiving visitors for obvious reasons. They are by this mode left at liberty to select the time of re-entering into society.

Morning visits should be made between the hours of twelve and two, and should be of short duration, say from five to fifteen minutes.

Between the hours above specified, the lady to whom the visit is paid should be prepared to receive her guests, if at home, *at once*, or direct her servant to say to them "*not at home,*" which is a mere conventional term, and means nothing more than that she cannot see them, and should not be construed into a mark of disrespect. It is impolite for her to keep her visitors long waiting, and appears as though she was not in the habit of receiving visits.

Should the lady to whom the visit is paid be preparing to go out, or to sit down to table, the visitor should leave almost immediately, notwithstanding the urgent request to remain. The lady visited should take good care not to show any surprise or discomfiture at an inopportune visit.

At some houses one or more days in each week are set apart for receiving morning visits. This custom has its advantages.

A card left at the house is all that is absolutely necessary in paying morning visits, even when the lady is at home, although some think it too formal. In Washington, this practice prevails to a greater extent than in the other cities, but it is found to be so useful, that it is daily becoming more general elsewhere.

A lady who *pays* a morning visit should do so in full street dress; this is only a proper respect shown to the friend whom she visits.

A lady receiving a morning visit should be clad neatly, but with simplicity; jewels are entirely out of place here.

All conversations about one's household affairs should be studiously avoided. Nothing is more vulgar than for the lady to entertain her guests with her domestic annoyances, or *her troubles about her servants.* The natural inference is that she is either boasting, which is always disgusting, or that she has not long been accustomed to her present household.

The internal machinery of a household, like that portion of the theatre, *"behind the scenes,"* should on this, as well as on every other occasion, be studiously kept out of view.

A gentleman should keep his hat in his hand during the visit, or at all events carry it with him into the reception room, as it indicates that he does not intend to remain long.

It is not proper to observe the gentleman's hat, or offer to put it away for him, as he can dispose of it very readily if he desires to do so.

If a lady meets a gentleman at the house of a friend, and desires to continue his acquaintance, her father or brother may call upon him, which he can return by a visit to the lady as well as to her male relatives.

If a gentleman is presented to a lady at an evening party in a proper manner, he is at liberty to call upon her soon after, although he may not have received a visit from her male connections. She is, of course, at liberty to make this acquaintance a slight or familiar one.

A lady may visit a public library and many other public places unattended by a gentleman, without the slightest breach of decorum. This custom is in general use in Washington, and to some extent in the other cities, which are day by day getting rid of the provincialism that suggested its impropriety.

In Boston, New York, Philadelphia and Baltimore, the principal public libraries are arranged with an eye to the visits of ladies, and in one at least, the Mercantile Library of Baltimore, containing nearly ten thousand volumes, the rooms during the early part of the day are expressly devoted to ladies, who attend in large numbers. The same may be said of the Fine Arts Exhibitions, under the patronage of Fine Art Societies, so deservedly popular in most of the large cities, a majority of whose patrons are *unattended ladies*. A concert or a theatre is another matter.

Ordinary evening visits imply a greater degree of intimacy, and must be regulated by the circumstances of the case. As a general rule, no evening visit should be made before eight o'clock, nor continue after ten.

New Year's Day Visits

THE practice prevails generally in New York, and partially in the other cities, of paying visits on New Year's day. The time of visiting on this day begins as early as ten o'clock and continues until three, or later. The lady remains at home to receive her visitors, who are usually gentlemen, and partakes of some refreshment with each, as wine and cake, or coffee, which is placed conveniently on a table.

Each visitor leaves his card, and remains but a few moments. The day furnishes an opportunity of healing up any estrangements or differences which may have arisen among friends, and is one of great hilarity.

A New Year's visit may be made within the week succeeding the first day of January.

If a lady does not receive visits, a servant should be in readiness to receive the cards of visitors.

When a gentleman has many visits to pay, he may leave his card at the door without going in.

In Washington it is the custom for the most distinguished public functionaries to hold public levées, which are visited by both ladies and gentlemen.

The Ball Room

PUBLIC balls or assemblies are usually under the direction of a board of managers selected for the occasion, under whose auspices the invitations sent out to the ladies, and tickets sold to the gentlemen, are placed. The intention ordinarily is to place such a guard over the admissions, as to bring together a society which shall not be displeasing to those present, but as by the purchase of a ticket a person of a different description may gain admission, notwithstanding the vigilance of the managers, they cannot be held responsible for the character of those present.

The managers usually select from their number a *"committee of arrangement,"* under whose direction the assembly is placed, and who represent the entertainers of the party, the others considering themselves, *with a qualification,* their guests.

It is the duty of this committee of arrangement to see that every thing is conducted with proper decorum; and as an entertainer is exceedingly anxious to contribute to the enjoyment of his guests, so the intercourse of this contribute to the enjoyment of his guests, so the intercourse of this committee, with the other members of the party, should be marked by the most studied politeness and anxiety to please. No appearance of authority should be assumed by them, and if any circumstance arises, needing their interference, it should be done so quietly as not to attract the attention of a single individual, beyond those concerned. Above all, no manifestation of temper should be exhibited under any provocation, and no person is fitted for such a position who has not a perfect control of himself.

It is highly impolite to ask a lady to dance, without an acquaintance, before being presented to her. She will most probably decline in such a manner as to convince the person making the request, of her appreciation of his rudeness.

If an entire stranger desires a partner for a dance, he must solicit an introduction from a member of the committee of arrangement, who will introduce him to any lady he points out, if there is no impropriety in so doing. At all events, it is his duty to procure for him a partner.

A lady is by no means compelled to dance with a stranger, if presented properly, but she is obliged to treat him with due courtesy. He has a right to demand a *polite*, and not a *cold refusal*.

A lady may decline to dance with an acquaintance, without its being considered a just cause of offence. A gentleman has the privilege of selecting his partner, and there is no reason why the lady should not exhibit her preference likewise.

The lady should be led through the figure with the utmost possible delicacy. Her partner has the privilege of taking her hand for this purpose, but he should not abuse the privilege. He should simply touch and not grasp it; and in waltzing, particular care should be taken to avoid pressing her waist. It ought only to be touched with the open hand.

It is polite to appear graceful rather than agile in the dance, and one should be particularly cautious about attempting much display in the steps or movements of the body.

A gentleman should always be present to fulfil a pervious engagement made to dance, lest he prevent the lady from joining the set, which is highly indecorous, and proves that he cares little for her.

After conducting his partner to a seat, a gentleman may converse with her for a few minutes, if she does not join the next set, but he must retire on the approach of another gentleman, unless he has a previous acquaintance. He should not attempt to seat himself beside her, without she request it, but remain standing.

It need hardly be said that full dress is the only one allowable in the ball room. Light gloves are the only ones admissible, and no *gentleman* will attempt to dance with ungloved hands.

A ball room acquaintance does not extend beyond the door of the room, and no one is justified in recognizing a lady whom he chances afterward to meet, without she bows first, and in that case only by raising the hat. If a more particular acquaintance is desired, it must be sought by means of a new and more formal introduction.

It is allowable for a gentleman to pay a visit of inquiry to a lady of his acquaintance the day after meeting her at a ball, provided their relations are intimate.

Public Amusements

IF a gentleman accompanies a lady to a public assembly, and occupies a seat beside her, etiquette does not require him to relinquish it, unless, as sometimes happens, the seat is expressly reserved for ladies. Should he yield it, it must be considered as an act of courtesy and not one of right, and should be so received; but in so doing to a stranger, he should consider how far he is compromitting (1) the courtesy due to the lady under his protection. If he observes a personal acquaintance, he cannot well avoid offering her his seat, which she should decline if it is possible to obtain even an inferior one elsewhere, and if not, accept it with some kind of polite expression, as "I am sorry to discommode (2) you."

If a gentleman visits a public assembly unaccompanied by a lady, he is entitled to his seat, except under these circumstances: if a lady be an elderly one, fills a higher position in society, or is placed in a manifestly unpleasant situation by his retaining his position, the usage of polite society require, that he should offer it to her, which she should accept with suitable acknowledgements. Her sex confers on her no privilege to be rude, or to receive a kindness, without making such return as in her power.

Should the gentleman offering the seat be one rendered venerable by age, or distinguished by position, a much stronger reason exists, for the lady, if younger, or his inferior, to desire not to inconvenience him, and she should remember that although she may avail herself of his offer, yet if it is wantonly done, there are eyes, even of her own sex, fixed on her, who will draw conclusions not very favorable to her good breeding.

Some ladies, from false notions of propriety, conceive that it is necessary for a gentleman who accompanies them to a crowded assemblage, to procure seats for them immediately, even at the expense of rude behavior, or perhaps personal altercation. There can be no possible impropriety, in the ladies remaining standing, even for many minutes, until seats are provided for them, by the politeness of the assembly, rather than the discourtesy of their attendant. Indeed it is considered a mark of "haut ton" (3) for a lady to appear somewhat independent under such circumstances, and not to exhibit an anxiety to shuffle herself into a seat, as hurriedly as possible.

Private Balls

A VERY common mode of entertaining friends among fashionable people is by giving evening parties, or balls. The season for these entertainments usually begins about the first of January, and terminates at the beginning of lent, or Ash Wednesday. Frequently evening parties are renewed after the cessation of lent.

The invitations are issued by the *lady*, and *not* the gentleman, and are sent out about one week previous to the entertainment. They may be printed or written. The length of time betwixt the issuing of the invitations, and the entertainment, usually indicates its pretensions. Engraved cards are now much used for this purpose, and are considered quite appropriate.

The gentleman may give a verbal invitation to a friend, but one so invited should take very good care to leave his card with the lady, previous to the evening of the party, lest she be not aware of the invitation, a card left in this mode will bring about an explanation betwixt herself and husband.

The guests are expected to assemble betwixt the hours of nine and ten, before which every preparation for their reception should be in readiness. It is better to employ a competent person to superintend the internal arrangement, than to leave it to chance, nothing is more ridiculous than at *attempt*. Better not to give the party at all, than an indifferent one. Its character will of course depend on the accommodations and amount of money expended, but let it be complete, of its kind.

During the early part of the evening the lady should be stationed in one position, in her drawing room, to receive her guests as they enter.

A lady may precede the gentleman in entering the drawing room, or lean upon his arm. Both should immediately approach the lady of the house and exchange salutations with her before recognizing any other person in the room, after which they should join their friends, and leave her free to receive new visitors.

It is the custom at some houses to announce the name of each guest as he or she enters the drawing room.

If the lady should not at the moment be seen, the guests may enter into conversation with any one whom they chance to know, and make their salutations on her return.

The lady entertaining should dance but little, in order that she may have time to attend to her guests but when she does so, she selects her own partner.

Either the hostess or her husband may begin the dance. If the lady, she selects her partner, who is honored by the act; if the gentleman, he chooses the most distinguished lady in the room for his partner.

When supper is announced, each gentleman offers his arm to a lady, and preceded by the host, and followed by the hostess, the party enters the supper room.

Gloves should be removed at supper, but kept on during the rest of the evening.

When refreshments are handed round the gentleman at whose house the ball is given should not accompany the servant, but leave the guests to provide themselves with such articles as they desire.

A lady should be permitted to help herself, without she requests a gentleman to do if for her, because she is the best to judge of her own taste.

It is impolite to place an empty glass or plate just used, upon a waiter containing refreshments. A servant should follow to collect these things.

Servants should occasionally be sent through the room to procure any little thing a guest may stand in need of, but it is impolite to call off a domestic when handing refreshments, to procure any article.

Card-tables are arranged either in a room set apart for that purpose, or in the drawing room, on each of which a fresh pack of cards should be placed. Those who are disposed to play draw a card from the pack, and all except the four lowest are excluded from the game. Betting is rarely practiced for any thing beyond a trifling amount at general parties, and then never by *ladies*.

It is in bad taste for a husband and wife to be much together in company, as they can enjoy each other's society at home. The purpose of mingling in general society is to enjoy that of others.

It any accident occurs it should pass unnoticed, especially by the entertainer. A lady who had suddenly sprang into affluence, gave a large party to her friends in her new house. During the evening a servant jostled the waiter on which he was carrying around refreshments, and overturned a large quantity of ice-cream, with other knick-knacks. This was too much for the good lady's philosophy, who exclaimed, "there goes the ice-cream over my new Turkey carpet;" and fell to the task of removing it with her own hands, infinitely to the amusement of her guests, and the mortification of her friends.

Guests should retire as quietly as possible, and without taking leave of their entertainers, who should not notice their departure, lest it break up the company.

Music

A SONG or two, or a piece, of music well performed at intervals, furnishes an agreeable relief to an assemblage, but when continued too long, so far from being agreeable, it degenerates into a source of annoyance.

A lady, when asked to sing, should do so at once, if she intends to sing at all. She should neither require great persuasion to induce her to begin, nor very decided hints to leave off. The sweetest toned voice loses its effect by repetition, an no lady can long fix the attention of an audience.

It is highly impolite to keep up a conversation while others are singing, for, besides the distraction it occasions to the person singing, it prevents others, with more refined taste, from listening.

One should be careful not to attempt the execution of a piece beyond his or her vocal powers. The singer should feel and express the sentiment of the song, if effect is desired, but all affectation is easily detected and ludicrous.

There is a great deal of ridiculous cant (4) about music, which every person who essays to good breeding should be careful to avoid. The truth is, that with the exception of an occasional opera at New York and New Orleans, and the Cathedral choir at Baltimore, we seldom hear music of the highest order in this country; and no individual who has heard two or three of the popular operas, performed by as many passable singers, with a meagre orchestra and an inferior chorus, can lay any claim to nice musical discrimination. The faculty of *appreciating* music requires cultivation for its development, and as yet we have but few schools to improve it, in this country. There are many things of which, as a nation, we may be justly proud, but music is not one of them.

Dress

THE dress of both the lady and gentleman is so much a mere matter of taste, and depends so greatly on the fashion of the moment, that it would be superfluous to prescribe any fixed to rule for it. There are certain proprieties, however, which no change of fashion can alter. Small matters, as well made shoes and gloves, and appropriate handkerchiefs, frequently discover the true lady and gentleman. About these the well bred person is always particular.

Every individual should dress in keeping with his circumstances, but no well bred person will desire to appear conspicuous on account of the extreme fashion or outlandishness of his dress.

It is due to society that its members should present a respectable appearance, but it is not dress alone which gives an individual a position in it. The more unassuming the dress, the more appropriate and respectable it is.

In full dress, a black dress coat and pantaloons, with either a black stain or light vest, are most suitable, although other colors are admissible.

A lady should be particular to select her dress with an eye to chasteness. Silky and pliable materials, which show the graceful contour of the female form, are more desirable than harsh unyielding ones.

A lavish display of jewelry, especially of a cheap kind, is improper. For the morning dress jewelry is out of place.

There are dresses appropriate for the house, street, and carriage, which vary with each change of fashion. A lady should be careful to use each in their appropriate place. She may be plainly clad in her carriage if she will, but not conspicuously appareled while walking.

The tailor and milliner have less to do with the formation of society than is generally imagined, and those who depend on such adventitious (5) circumstances for their position, will sooner or later discover how unstable was the foundation on which they had built. It is true that in every country the possession and lavish expenditure of money will bestow on its possessor a certain consideration, which without other qualities will be a very doubtful one. Much as the Americans are accused of their adoration at the shrine of mammon, we think we hazard nothing in the assertion, that money — mere money — will procure less consideration in the United States, than in any civilized country on the globe.

In a commercial community like the United States, however, where fortunes are rapidly acquired and as suddenly lost, society is ever changing, and those who were quietly plodding their way yesterday, are elevated on its waves to-day. This elevation is and should be the aim and ambition of every American citizen, provided he endeavors to qualify himself, not by mere money, but by striving to refine his mind and elevate his character, for an exaltation of his position. One of the chief objects of this work is to assist him in this endeavor,

Gloves

GLOVES should always be worn at church and other public assemblages, as the theatre and opera.

Ladies occasionally wear gloves at dinner. This is exceedingly bad taste, and should never be done, except to conceal some defect of the hands.

When meeting a lady, a gentleman should not stop to unglove before shaking hands, especially if his hand be moist with perspiration. It is awkward for both parties to be kept standing for some moments while this operation is effected, and destroys the frankness and ease which is supposed to prompt this mode of salutation.

It is a frequent custom for ladies when about to walk or drive, to draw on their gloves while leaving the street door. This is highly improper; the toilet should be full and complete before leaving the dressing room.

The color of gloves is subject to much caprice, and is regulated by the reigning fashion of the moment. At an evening party or the opera, however, black gloves are never admissible, even in mourning, except perhaps in the case of clergymen, or physicians. White, or exceedingly light gloves, are here always to be worn.

Funerals

PRINTED invitations are frequently sent to such friends as the family desire to attend the funeral, in the event of the decease of one of its members. Those to the more intimate should be written. Invitations may with propriety be dispensed with altogether; there is no fixed rule on this subject.

The friends of the deceased may accompany the remains to their last resting place, or leave at the house. In Washington, those who go in their own carriages, accompany the procession until it reaches Capitol Hill, when they leave it or continue at their option.

Visits of condolence should not be made before ten days after the funeral.

Return cards for these visits intimate that the family are again prepared to receive their friends, and the time for sending them must be left to the option of the family.

Notes and letters should be sealed with black sealing wax, during the entire period of mourning.

Jewelry is out of place with mourning apparel. Furs, in the season, are appropriate, especially the darker ones, for ladies.

Visiting Cards

A FAMILY, on arriving in town, after an absence of some time, should send their cards to their acquaintances.

When the visit is intended for more than one member of the family, separate cards should be left, especially if there be two married sisters, or a guest. The lady may leave her husband's card.

In leaving a card for a friend who is at the house of a person with whom you have no acquaintance, be careful not to write his name on it, else it may be construed into a mark of disrespect towards the family with whom he is tarrying.

The mother and daughters may leave their names on one card, but no daughter's name should be left, who is not already "brought out," or who does not intend to make her appearance during the season.

A lady who intends to give a formal ball or party, should leave cards with those whom she intends to invite, one or two weeks previous to the issue of cards of invitation.

If an invitation of any kind is given to a person whom the inviter has never visited, it should be accompanied by his or her card.

After a wedding the cards of both the bride and bridegroom are sent around to their acquaintances, to inform them of the wish of the newly married pair to continue their acquaintance. The parents of the bride send out the cards to their acquaintances, and the bridegroom sends them to his. They may be enclosed in an envelope, but should never be tied by a white ribbon, as is sometimes done.

Cards left at the residence of the bride, should be answered by cards notifying them when she will be prepared to receive a visit.

In Washington it is *not* considered disrespectful to send a card by a servant, to return a visit. In the other cities the custom does not prevail to any extent. It is better, however, to leave it in person, everywhere, if convenient so to do.

When an individual of family are about to be absent for some time, they should announce the fact to their friends by leaving a card with the letters P. P. C., *(pour prendre congée,)* (6) or T. T. L., *(to take leave,)* written upon it.

Marriage

A BACHELOR'S acquaintances have no right to consider themselves such after his marriage, unless he intimates a wish to continue the acquaintance by sending his card, together with that of his intended bride, to them, or personally requests a continuance, and no offence should be taken by not being numbered among his newly selected friends; for a gentleman has as undoubted right to make a selection of such persons as he considers suitable associates for him as a married man, and he has furthermore an equally undoubted privilege of living as retired as he choses, on both of which points he is certainly the best judge.

It is perhaps better for a bachelor to give a dinner to his friends at parting, in order to show that his discontinuance of *intimacy* arises from no improper feeling.

Married Life

ONE of the holiest and most sacred of shrines, is that which finds its abode by the domestic fireside, provided it is preserved in its purity. Society may be agreeable or disagreeable, and yet not furnish its participants more than momentary enjoyment or pain. Not so with the domestic circle. For weal or for woe, it is inseparably connected with the long hours of those who compose it, — it is their life of pleasure or of pain. How vicious must that heart then be, which will light the face with a smile and clothe the lips with gentle words in society, only to exhibit itself in society, only to exhibit itself in the privacy of this circle, in a gloomy, fretful, and ill-natured disposition. No matter how lovely the form, or angelic the face, they cannot conceal the source from whence all this evil springs.

"Some flow'rest of Eden ye still inherit,
But the trail of the serpent is over them all."

In the formation of matrimonial alliances, it is necessary to use the greatest care to ascertain that there be a similarity in social position, in thought, sentiment, refinement, education, intelligence and disposition, for without all these pre-requisites, and they are unfortunately too often overlooked, marriage will entail misery instead of furnishing unalloyed happiness.

There is no reason why persons living in the same house should be less observant of ceremony than among strangers. It is true, that in the privacy of domestic life, many of the more studied forms of etiquette are dispensed with, but none which interfere with true politeness or good breeding.

If a husband and wife, think each other unworthy of the bestowal of these attentions, there will not long remain even the semblance of respect.

Among the most refined class of society, it is usual, when the house will admit of it, for the husband and wife to have separate dressing rooms, and neither should perform before the other, those duties of the toilet, which though necessary, might offend a delicate sensibility.

On meeting at the breakfast table, or for the first time in the morning, each individual should salute the other with the customary salutations they would apply to guests, and with studied politeness.

It is the height of rudeness for a lady to appear slovenly at this or any other time, and evinces not only a want of respect for those she may be thrown in contact with, but an innate vulgarity of mind. The dress may be exceedingly simple, but should be neat, and the hair carefully arranged. There is something excessively disgusting to a refined person, in the idea of a half made toilet, especially if the person offending be a female.

The conversation of a family circle is more familiar, and less studied, than that used in the formal intercourse of society, but it should be equally marked by politeness and freedom from any thing which may render it unpleasant. Innuendos, or double meanings, which are the demons of private life should be avoided, as the promptings of the evil one. A good rule is so to conduct conversation, that the entrance of a stranger need not interrupt it, nor change its tone.

A lady cannot be too particular in her domestic arrangements, especially those which conduce (7) to the comfort of her husband. It is her province to preside over her household, and she should discharge this duty with great scrupulousness, yet without bustle or a display of temper.

The table may be simple, and the fare homely, yet is should be arranged with the utmost possible neatness, and in such a manner as not to disturb them if a great unexpectedly drops in. On such an occasion, no excuses are necessary even for a plain dinner, as the circumstances, will explain themselves, and any allusion to them in the way of an apology is considered ill bred.

With proper management a lady, by personal superintendence, if she has not a housekeeper, for a short time each morning, even with a small number of servants, may have a well ordered household, without the performance of any of its drudgery.

No matter how exalted her position she cannot possibly detract from it, by understanding the arrangement of her domestic affairs, and even taking part in the preparation of those little delicacies of the table, which few servants readily comprehend, without careful instructions from their mistress. An accomplished lady may well be proud of the delicacy and taste of the arrangements of her table.

In the management of servants, while no approach is made to familiarity, it should be remembered that they have sensibilities as well as their employers, and should be treated with mildness. Their manners will assimilate insensibly to those with whom they live.

Conversation

THE soul of society is conversation, and he who has not at least some pretensions to conversational powers, no matter what other qualifications he may possess, is fitted to perform a very poor part in it. It is true, that every one is not gifted with the same intellectual capacity, or colloquial powers, but with the attention to a few simple rules, each person may contribute somewhat towards the gratification of those in whose company he chances to be placed.

The great art of conversation is not only to interest the listener in the subject, but likewise to induce him to engage in it. A conversation in which each individual finds himself irresistibly engaged, acts like sparkling champagne, by enlivening the spirits of all who partake of it.

There are many learned persons who show badly in society for the want of the discrimination and tact necessary to keep up a conversation which shall elicit the views of those with whom they converse, as well as display their own mental ability. Hence, nothing is more common than to be greatly disappointed in a truly great man, when met for the first time in society.

It is exceedingly rude not to pay attention to a conversation addressed to yourself. If you are not interested, seize a proper opportunity for breaking it off in a polite manner.

An argument should never be carried on in a general company. No individual is bound to correct the false opinions another may entertain, and if slight inaccuracies occur, it is far better to allow them to pass, than to attempt their correction.

No consideration will justify a loss of command over the temper, and every person should remember, that is he does not owe it to the society in which he is placed, he at least does to himself, to preserve his equanimity. Passion is even more objectionable in a lady than a gentleman.

Prolixity (8) is always tiresome. One should endeavor to acquire the habit of condensing his thoughts into the fewest words, and relate only such points of a subject as are prominent, without going into detail, lest he get the reputation of a bore.

Courtesy is a distinctive characteristic of gentility; and stiffness and hauteur of the want of it. A polished person is always an agreeable companion, not only for his equals, but his *inferiors*.

A loud tone of voice and a boastful manner should be carefully avoided. A modest person is sure to be appreciated, and a boastful one laughed at in his absence.

One of the great merits of conversation is, to be intelligible and pertinent. The simplest language, and that which most directly approaches the point, is best.

It requires a peculiar faculty to relate an anecdote with effect, and he who has it not, should never make himself ridiculous by attempting a part for which nature has not fitted him. Many great men are wanting in this particular, while many shallow ones possess this faculty in an eminent degree.

Family matters should never form the subject of conversation. The good qualities of one's children may be very interesting to the parents, but cannot possibly much entertain another person. If enquiry is made concerning them, of a mother, she may speak of them and turn at once to another subject.

The difficulty of managing servants is a fruitful topic of conversation with many ladies, and always out of place. It is better, as a general rule, never to mention the name of servant, nor make the least allusion to domestic arrangements. Depend upon it, others do not care for them.

To be a good listener is an important as to be a good talker, and frequently more difficult, because most men are fonder of giving their own suggestions than of listening to those of others.

Drawing rooms frequently contain paintings and statuary, and a cabinet for bijouterie (9), or small articles of value. There is no impropriety in looking at these, as they are placed there for that purpose; besides, they are frequently suggestive topics of conversation. A painting or statue may have its story, and the little articles of raw workmanship, their anecdote or remembrance. A lady may with propriety call the attention of her visitors to any article of this kind, not on account of its price, which would display *vulgarity*, but of its beauty, or rarity, which would manifest *taste*.

An article of furniture or dress may likewise be admired on the same principle, but no allusion should be made to its cost, nor should the visitor ask from whence it was obtained. The possessor may voluntarily give that information if she chooses.

Especial care should be taken not to speak in the disparagement of an absent person. It is low bred to take advantage of absence to say what dare not be told directly to the person; besides, although the curiosity of those present may be gratified, they will be certain to hold in little esteem the person who contributes in this manner to their entertainment.

An insult should never be resented, nor even recognized, in company. If the person to whom it is given is a truly brave one, he will choose the appropriate moment for redress.

The name of a person with whom another is conversing, should never be repeated. No one desires to hear his name called over and over from the lips of another, unless it is necessary to call his attention.

The person at whose house the company is, should not take the lead in conversation. He should suggest topics if no one else does, and when it is fairly under way, leave it for the entertainment of others, taking care to supply any deficiency that may occur.

Dinner

GUESTS to a dinner are necessarily introduced to each other. No one should be invited, therefore, who would not be perfectly agreeable to the others.

As a general rule, the invitations should be confined to those who have a similarity of thought, or if an exception be made, it should be in favor of persons of greater distinction.

The number of guests should be so arranged that neither two ladies or gentlemen will be forced to sit together, and their disposition at the table should have an eye to this successive alternation of lady and gentleman.

The time for issuing the invitations before the entertainment, varies. One week is probably the most appropriate period, but it may with propriety range from two to fourteen days. The invitation should specify the *precise hour of dining.* This may be either four, five, six or seven o'clock, P. M., five is the usual hour.

An invitation to dinner invariably requires an immediate answer, accepting or declining, and should be addressed to the lady. It is a piece of unpardonable rudeness to neglect a reply. After accepting an invitation to dine, should any circumstance occur to prevent the fulfilment of the obligation, the hostess should be immediately apprised of it.

In order to have a dinner pass off properly, every thing necessary must be provided in advance, and the whole placed under the superintendence of an experienced domestic.

A waiter should be provided for every guests, each of whom should have a white napkin in his hand, to place between his thumb and the plate he serves. Some wear white gloves, but this practice is not considered in as good taste as the white napkin.

Punctuality is of the greatest importance in attending a dinner. The guests should arrive neither too early nor too late, but *at the exact moment.* It is unpardonable to keep a company waiting beyond the appointed time.

It is proper for the host or hostess, after the guests have assembled, to point out to each gentleman what lady he is expected to escort to the dinner table, and even to assign each a seat at the table; but where this is not done, when dinner is announced, each gentleman offers his arm to a lady, and, preceded by the host, follows to the dining room. The hostess invariably enters the room after all her guests, and is escorted by one of the most distinguished gentlemen present.

It is considered the very height of good breeding for an entertainer to mingle with his guests as one of them, and not to indicate by word or look, a difference. With a sufficient number of well trained servants, and a plentiful table, this can be readily accomplished. It is truly surprising what freedom and hilarity such a demeanor on the part of the entertainer gives to the entire party, and what stiffness and restraint are imposed upon them, by the ill concealed anxiety of the host or hostess. Beneath this mask of nonchalance, care should be taken to see that each guest is well cared for, but in such a manner as not to attract notice.

A husband and wife, or near members of the same family, should never sit together at a dinner.

The gentleman in whose house the dinner is given, takes his place at the lower end of the table, and his lady at the upper: on either side of him are the two most distinguished ladies. Sometimes the host and hostess are seated opposite to each other in the middle of the table.

An entertainment begins with soup, a *small portion* of which is placed before each guest. If he does not desire it, he can allow it to remain untouched, but it is not proper to ask a second time for soup, except at a family dinner.

Soup is succeeded by fish, which should be helped with a silver fish-knife. These two services are in reality but the prelude to the dinner, which follows them.

Carving should be performed at a side table. If, however, an individual is requested to carve a dish, he should do it seated, and if he does not feel competent, he may with propriety decline.

Gravy should be placed at the side of the plate, and not over the meat and vegetables, and in small quantity.

In helping to a dish, it is impolite to load the plate with any one thing, and if it be a rarity, it should be served with discretion, in order that all may partake of it. Wherever it can be done in helping, a spoon should be used instead of a knife and fork.

The business of a knife is to divide the food, and not to eat with. The fork should invariably be used for this purpose. There can arise no circumstance which would justify a person in carrying his food to his mouth with a knife. The fork may be assisted in its office by a piece of bread, held between the thumb and finger of the left hand.

Napkins and silver forks are in such general use that no person would think of giving a dinner without them.

It is not the custom to ask ladies to take wine. Each lady is helped by the gentleman who sits next her, but no wine is circulated before the fish is eaten.

It is usual to drink the same wine with the person who requests you to pledge his health, but this practice is not invariable.

It is impolite to refuse to take wine with any person who requests it. The glass may be simply put to the lips.

When an article is sent by the host, it is not necessary to wait until others are helped before proceeding to eat.

The host and hostess retain their plates until their guests have finished their course.

The plate is changed with each course, as well as the knife and forks, which should be placed on it when the guest has finished the course.

Finger glasses, with water, and two or three slices of lemon in each, are brought in with the dessert.

It is impolite *to order* servants at the table of another, *request* them in a mild manner, to serve you to what you need.

It is not proper to collect a large mass of refuse around your plate. It is better to ask a servant to bring a plate on which to place and remove it.

Coffee may be served at the dinner table after dessert, but it should not come on to soon. When gentlemen sit at wine after the ladies retire, it is served in the drawing room. Some consider it more proper to serve it always in the drawing room, but this is a matter of taste.

The hostess gives the signal for the termination of dinner by rising. The gentlemen rise with the ladies, and if they continue at table after them, remain standing until they have left the room, when they reseat themselves.

The entertainer should neither make apologies for, nor praise the dinner. It is there—so let it pass; and if any thing goes amiss, let no notice be taken of it.

Each guest owes a visit to the hostess during the week following the entertainment, which it is impolite not to pay.

Invitations, Notes and Letters

AS a chief object of this volume is to instruct those who do *not* know the customary forms of society, it has been thought proper to append the following observations on notes, letters, &c.

A letter or note should be written on unruled paper, (white is preferable) and if addressed to a gentleman, his name in the superscription (10) should terminate with Esq., unless he has a title, which should be given in its stead.

White envelopes, are now generally used, together with sealing wax, which is considered more respectful than a wafer.

The following was the form of invitation to dinner adopted by President Madison:

"Mr. Madison requests the pleasure of Mr. Randolph's company at dinner, on Tuesday next, at 7 o'clock."

"Thursday, February 12th."

A note of this kind requires an *immediate reply*, which may be couched in the following terms and addressed to the *lady:*

"Mr. Randolph has the honor to acknowledge the receipt of Mr. Madison's note, inviting him to dine on Tuesday next, at 7 o'clock, and takes great pleasure in accepting the invitation."

Or,

"Mr. Randolph has the honor to acknowledge the receipt of the President's note, inviting him to dine on Tuesday next, at 7 o'clock, and regrets that a severe indisposition, which confines him to his room, will prevent his acceptance of the invitation."

"Saturday, February 14th."

A husband and wife may be included in the same note of invitation, but if other members of a family are invited, it is perhaps advisable to send separate invitations.

An invitation to an evening party should always be sent in the name of the lady, and does not require an answer, thus,

"Mrs. Hunter requests the pleasure of Mr. and Mrs. Almont's company, on Thursday evening, 15th instant."

"Monday, March 5th."

This may be written or printed.

Notes of the above description are intended for dinners and evening parties of the most formal kind. When others of less pretensions are given, it may prevent disappointment by including in the note some explanation, thus,

"Mr. R. would be happy to have the company of Mr. and Mrs. T. at a dinner to-morrow, 'en famille.' (11) The dining hour is 4 o'clock."

"Wednesday."

Or.

"Mr. R. would be happy to have the company of Mr. and Mrs. G. at dinner to-morrow, to meet Dr. H.

"But two or three other guests are expected. The dining hour is 4 o'clock."

"Monday Morning."

An invitation to spend an evening, may be written, thus,

"Mrs. D. would be pleased to see Mr. H. on Wednesday evening. A small company only is expected."

"Monday Morning."

Or,

"Miss R. would be pleased to see Mr. and Mrs. W. on to-morrow evening, at a small whist party."

"Friday Morning."

In addressing a lady, a gentleman should be careful to use the most respectful terms.

"Mr. R. presents his compliments to Miss C. and begs her acceptance of the accompanying slight present."

"Wednesday, May 15."

A lady may with propriety address a gentleman, thus,

"Miss R's compliments to Mr. D. and would feel much indebted to him for the loan of the volume he was speaking of last evening."

Many of these forms may seem so familiar as to appear trifling, but if they assist one well meaning person, in escaping from a dilemma, in which the want of early advantage may have placed him or her, they will not have been written in vain.

General Observations

A GENTLEMAN who meets a lady of his acquaintance in the street, should always raise his hat from his head, in recognizing her, and not simply *touch* it.

If a gentleman meets an acquaintance in company with a lady who is unknown to him, he should raise his hat from his head in passing.

The hat should be taken off in handing a lady from or to her carriage, or indeed in bestowing any similar attention upon her.

At a place of public amusement, it is polite for a gentleman, who is casually engaged in conversation with a lady, to retire on the approach of another, unless there is some obvious reason for detaining him.

In escorting ladies to a place of public amusement, the gentlemen usually precede them in entering the room.

In visiting it is improper to take the chair usually occupied by the lady or gentleman of the house, even if offered, unless the relations of the are so friendly as to cause them to dispense with formality.

In receiving visits, if but one guest is in the room, it is proper to accompany him to the street door, on his departure, if however there are guests left in the room, a servant should be directed to perform that office.

In a drawing room, it is better not to cross the room simply for the purpose of bowing to a lady of your acquaintance, and if you desire to engage in conversation with her, so arrange it that the meeting shall appear accidental. This is the more necessary if her position be an elevated one in society.

It frequently occurs that a lady desires to entertain her friends, without the formality or expense of a ball or evening party. On such an occasion it is better to give them a verbal invitation; which may be delivered in person or through a servant, stating precisely what sort of a *"soirée"* is expected.

If invitations are written, they should not be sent before the day prior to the one on which the entertainment is to be given, and should state the character of the *"soirée."*

Such an entertainment may be considered in the light of an evening visit, at which the guests would assemble, if the hour was not specified, at eight. The dress appropriate here would not be so at an "evening party."

Professional gentlemen are excused from many of those strict observances of etiquette, which might interfere with more important duties.

THE END.

End Notes

1. Compromitting — to make a promise or pledge by an act or declaration.
2. Discommode — to cause someone trouble or inconvenience.
3. Haut Ton — 19th-century slang for people of high fashion.
4. Cant — denoting a phrase or catchword current or in fashion.
5. Adventitious — happening or carried on according to chance rather than design.
6. *Pour Prendre Congée* — in English the phrase translates to "paid parting call."
7. Conduce — to help bring about a particular situation or outcome.
8. Prolixity — a person given to speaking at great or tedious length.
9. Bijouterie — jewelry or trinkets.
10. Superscription — the address line on a letter.
11. *En Famille* — in English the phrase translates to "in family."

Suggested Reading

Halttunen, Karen. *Confidence Men and Painted Women: A Study of Middle-Class Culture in America, 1830-1870.* New Haven: Yale University Press, 1982.
Kasson, John F. *Rudeness & Civility: Manners in Nineteenth-Century Urban America.* New York: Hill and Wang, 1990.

THE SALUTATION.

About The Author

Michelle L. Hamilton earned her master's degree in history from San Diego State University in 2013. She is a lifelong student of history.

Michelle's other works include: *"I Would Still Be Drowned In Tears"* Spiritualism in Abraham Lincoln White House.

"My Heart Is In The Cause" The Civil War Diary of James Meyers – Hospital Steward 45th Pennsylvania 1863-1865

Hamilton currently serves as the manager of the Mary Washington House Museum in Fredericksburg, VA. She is not new to historical house museums as she also worked as a docent at The Whaley House Museum in Old Town San Diego from 2001 until 2006.

She has been a Civil War living historian for over a decade participating in Civil War living history events around California and Virginia. Additionally, she has been a requested speaker at several Civil War Roundtable meetings, radio talk shows and numerous magazine publications including "The Citizen's Companion"

See her list of other publications and request a copy from her website: www.MichelleLHamilton.net

Enjoy her blog at: http://michelle-hamilton.blogspot.com